MW01172644

Cooking it old School & Ministry

Lossie Dupree

Cooking it old School & Ministry

Copyright @ 2021 by Lossie Dupree.

All Rights Reserved.

All rights reserved. No part of this publication may be reproduced, distributed, or transmitted in any form or by any means, including photocopying, electronic or mechanical methods, without the prior written permission of the copyright owner and the publisher of this book, except in the case of brief quotations embodied in critical reviews and certain other noncommercial uses permitted by copyright law. For permission requests, send an email to the copyright owner.

Email: lossiedupree@gmail.com

Quantity sales. Special discounts are available on quantity purchase by corporations, associations, and others. For details, contact the publisher at lossiedupree@gmail.com

Orders by U.S. trade bookstores and wholesalers, please contact Lossie Dupree: Tel: (252) 382-0900 or Email: lossiedupree@gmail.com

Printed in the United States of America.

Publishing, Book Design, Layout & Editing by MBT Marketing Solutions & Associates, Owner Marilyn Bryant Tucker, MBA, EGBA & Doctoral Studies

Book Cover Photo Credit: Delano Brooks Owner of Artographic Canvas - Tarboro, North Carolina

Dedication

I would like to dedicate this book to my late Parent's Lillie Bryant (Lil) & James Bryant (Jim). I loved them dearly and will always cherish all the precious memories of love, wisdom, and support that we shared together.

In memory of my late sister Deputy Lillie Bea Knight, my nephew Ray Cherry, my niece Great Latoya Forte, and my best friend Mrs. Irene Vines Brown. All of whom I have loved. They were precious to me.

Acknowledgement

To my oldest daughter Marilyn Bryant-Tucker, thank you for your constant support and prayers while helping me write this book.

Additionally, a thank you to my youngest daughter Sandra Bryant Richardson, my oldest daughter Teresa Bryant McCalop, my grands, my son-in laws, my family, and my brother in Christ Benjamin Tyson. Most of all thank you to my God Almighty whom I give all the glory Honor and Praise.

Table of Contents

Introduction

~

C*ooking it Old School & Ministry* is designed to share wisdom and some of the delicious old-school dishes that my late Mother Lillie Mae Bryant better known as Lil shared and instilled in me. As you begin to read you will understand how much I appreciate the legacy that my late mom left behind so that I can share with others. Many old-fashioned dishes can be prepared with very few ingredients and still comes out flavorful.

The objectives:

- To turn a food that is implied to be not good into something delicious

- Not overlooking health issues

- To make cooking fun

- To appreciate the legacy of recipes

- To keep the word in the kitchen. Proverbs 22:6 "Rejoice Always."

- To make God's word lead and guide us in everything that we do. I Corinthians 10:31 "Whether therefore ye eat, or drink, or whatsoever ye do, do all to the Glory of God."

This book will help us to understand how to take a little something and turn it into a lot. Additionally, it will help us to turn (different) foods into delicious dishes, to cut corners on expenses while the ministry in the kitchen will help uplift your spirit and help make cooking fun and exciting.

Some of my old school dishes that I prepare, people with health issues can eat and enjoy fixing them.

Cooking it Old School & Ministry will take many of the senior citizens of today through memory lane. This book will instruct you to create many old recipes without a lot of spices, seasonings, and ingredients while still cooking delicious meals.

The ministry in the kitchen will help you concentrate on giving God thanks and praise to be able to prepare food for the table, when so many do not have that luxury.

What you will Learn:

- How to cook certain old school foods

- What to cook when you have health issues that restrict what you can eat

- What seasoning or oil is best to use

- How many ingredients to use on certain foods

- Portion control of foods being prepared

Why one should read this book:

- To learn more about old school dishes

- To learn how to use less ingredients

- To learn how to cook some old school dishes and a few desserts

- To learn how to enjoy cooking and ministry in the kitchen
- Appreciate the legacy of old school cooking

This guide was written to prepare the readers mind on how to understand and take advantage of cooking and ministry in the kitchen. This guide will help you to prepare delicious meals while also uplifting your spirit through giving God the praise.

History of Old School Foods

Psalm 146:7 "He upholds the cause of the oppressed and give food to the hungry."

Numerous things have contributed to old school cooking such as people, places, and different cultures. Old school foods have placed a great influence in many countries. Old school foods consist of many different animals, vegetables, and fruits. Southern states place great emphasis on old school foods. The three major cultures to consider are Native American, West African, and European.

The Native Americans were the one who introduced corn to the early settlers of America and was passed on to slave workers out in the fields. Corn is now most used for cornbread and hoecakes. The preservation of salting and frying meat was another skill passed on by Native Americans to the slaves. The salt was a way to keep the meats from going bad, which helped prevent spoiling or what some called skippers from getting into the meat, this also helped keep some people alive.

The West African Slaves brought an unknown vegetable that no one in the New World had heard of this was Okra and a meal cooked and stewed in a pot what we today call gumbo. Georgian Shrimp and Grits is the biggest influence the West Africans had on our old school dishes.

The Europeans introduced pork to the south and other parts of the country. They brought the first pig to the states. Pork became immensely popular increasing demand. When it comes to southern meals pork became exceedingly popular. The culture of BBQ was born in the south.

Greens such as collards were considered as an icon.

A lot of these green vegetables had to be prepared to prevent them from being poisonous. A technique called Meticulous Preparations was a technique in which one cooked the poison right out. Old school cooking is special because of the people who cook it and because of its culture that continues to preserve it. Its roots run strong and deep.

Preparation for Cooking

~

**Psalm 107:9 "The hungry soul He fills
with good things."**

I grew up on a sharecropper's farm in the deep country of Whitakers, North Carolina. We lived in a two- bedroom old wooden house, near a pond. The kitchen was exceedingly small and especially cold in the winter. We were extremely poor in materialistic; however, we were immensely rich spiritually. To get water for our food, bath, or essentials we either had to use a well or a sprout discovered by my uncle. When using the well, a bucket had to be dipped down connected with a rope to pull the water up. Finally, we did what you might call moved up and my uncle found a waterspout in the ground and there he built a pump where we had to pump the handle to get water; my uncle Juke was an expert at this. The only problem was if it did not rain much in the summer the pump would run dry and in the cold winter it would freeze therefore resulting in no water. My mom would always save some water in the kitchen and put it in a pot on the iron cooking stove, and let it boil. When the water was boiling, she would go outside and pour the hot water down the mouth of the pump to thaw the spout that had frozen. We all played a part in gathering up the wood for the stove for my mom to cook our meals. The stove even had an oven! Mom would always keep a pan of hot dishwashing water on the stove the entire time, even before cooking got started. She used a dish rag in the hot box lye soap water.

Foods Grown and Raised on the Farm

Matthew 5:6 "Who hunger and thirst for righteousness for they will be filled."

When harvest time for crops came, we shucked the peanuts by hand and lined them up headfirst on polls. Any peanuts left on the ground would be gathered up for personal consumption. We would fry them, boil them and even use them as toppings on cakes. Melted butter, sugar, and crushed peanuts cooked together for a frosting on what mom called a sweet bread pudding. Additionally, we often made peanut brittle for candy.

We raised our own chickens. Hens were used to lay eggs, and roosters were used for mating. Additionally, we raised hogs, which were used for lard, frying foods, meats such as porkchops, ribs, pigs' feet, ham, hog liver, and even the tongue. The hams and ribs from the hogs were used for BBQ. My dad and other men would kill, clean, make a fire, and sometimes cook an entire whole hog all at once. After they were done cooking the hog, they would cut it up and put the meat in a wooden tub.

Mom would use her homemade vinegar and red crushed seasoning; it would be so flavorful. Cole slaw would be made to go with BBQ, Mom made cole slaw from the cabbages grown in our garden. We had a smoke house where dad would put shoulders cut from hog prior to covering them with plenty of salt and some with a little syrup. The salt helped prevent them from spoiling.

Gifts My Grandpa Gave Me as a Child

John 4:34 "Jesus said to them, is to do the will of him who sent me my food."

My grandpa would always give me either a pig or chicks for my birthday every year as a child. The pigs and chicks became my pets. I became so attached to them, I always made sure they were fed and taken care of. As time progressed, little did I know that my pets would someday be food on the table. Sadly, that day came sooner than expected or wanted. I cried until I had no more tears to cry, I was so hurt that my first pet pig called Bo. I begged my dad to not kill him, but dad explained to me that to me that this pig was to be food for the family. When Bo was killed and cooked for BBQ, I was so devastated and hurt that I did not eat the meat because Bo was my pet. Years later some of my chickens were traded to a man who came by each week selling snacks who would take a trade if you did not have the money. This made me immensely sad. I cried and cried while my parents continued to remind me that this was necessary for survival. I learned to accept what was happening to my pets that I loved so dearly. There were many days filled with disappointment and hardships, but we stuck together through it all. We shared so much love for each other and every family on that sharecropper's farm supported and helped one another to make ends meet. Additionally, we shared clothes as much as we shared food.

Living near a pond had many pros, such as the fish being a main source of food for meals. At the pond we caught cod, perch, and bass. The cod fish were so huge, dad had to cut them up with an ax. Their meat was so fleshy, it did not really taste like fish.

Cooking and Ministry with Mom in the Kitchen

Matthew 4:4 "Man shall not live by bread alone but on every word that comes from the mouth of God."

The kitchen would be so cold, especially in the winter but there I was excited and ready to watch mom cook, hear her sing, and praising God while firing the stove up, getting it ready to cook our meal. There I watched her take flour, lard, and sour milk and watch her mix it together for homemade biscuits. These biscuits were famous with our fatback meat and molasses. Next, comes our eggs that were produced by our own chickens. Mom would love to sing the Lord will make a way somehow, I love the Lord and so many spiritual songs and just talking with mom in the kitchen. The adults had coffee and the children had Kool- Aid, water, or milk when someone milked a cow. Every so often mom would brew tea. Mom had a clean, thin cloth after the tea was brewed, she would put a cloth over a jar and add water, while mixing in sugar for drinking purposes. Sometimes we had butter, there was an old lady on the farm that milked the owner's cows, she would take the milk skim the top off the milk put separate and give it to us, then I would take the skim off the milk shake it in a clean jar till butter forms give it to mom. Mom would then add salt and put it in patties for us to eat with the homemade biscuits that she cooked. Before we eat, saying grace was a must, it was a tradition and required. If grace was not said, then you did not eat.

Mom would always say we have a lot to be thankful for. The only thing that mom was cautious with me about in the kitchen was not to get burned with the hot lard and boiling water. Every meal that mom cooked came out perfect and was always delicious. The children had a long bench behind the table to sit on the adults had chairs to sit in at the kitchen table to eat. We had very few choices of food, we ate whatever was placed on our plates and never questioned or complained. Rice, chicken, pork, vegetables, and grown fruits were some of the main things we had on our farm. Perch's, Cobs, and Bass fish caught in the pond was our main source of meals.

Mom never used many spices for the simple reason we could not afford them. Mom made her own BBQ Sauce. She passed the recipe down to me. The recipe consists of salt, black pepper and crushed red pepper. Mom will always be a great inspiration in my life.

My Very First Meal that I Cooked as a Child

Revelation 3:20 "If anyone hears my voice and opens the door, I will come in and eat with him and he will eat with me."

When I was a youth, I went with mom and dad fishing one day, where there were a bunch of us fishing together at the pond on the farm that day. When we finished fishing, mom told me to take the fish home and she would be home soon. Our mothers on the farm had this tradition, they sometimes would walk with one another home, that day I tried surprising mom by having dinner ready before she got home. I cleaned the fish as I had watched mom and dad. I pilled the white potatoes, made the fire, song and prayed as mom would do. Finally, I had gotten the fish scaled and cleaned. I sliced the white potatoes. I put lard in the pans to fry the fish. As the fish started getting finished on one side, I flipped it over to the uncooked side in the hot lard. Next, I started sprinkling salt and meat over them which was backwards. I was so excited about surprising my mom that I forgot to put the salt and meal on first. I did the white potatoes the same way. Mom came in at that time and I thought she would be angry, but she just smiled and helped me correct my mistake.

My First Meal I Cooked as an Adult

Matthew 4:4 "Man shall not live by bread alone, but by every word that comes from the mouth of God."

The very first dish that I cooked as an adult was a meat loaf in the oven, that was baked in a gas stove. I had fresh ground beef, chopped onions, black pepper, salt, little crumbled bread, and bell pepper mixing it well and then putting it in a square. I set the oven to 350 degrees and had my tomato sauce ready. A little before the meatloaf was done, I mixed sugar, bell peppers, onions tomato sauce together and poured the ingredients over the entire meatloaf until all ingredients was done. The meatloaf came out delicious. I cooked Cabbages with fat back meat. Cooked corn on the cobb and bake sweet potatoes.

Cooking Old School Soul Food in a Healthy Way

Matthew 6:11 "Give us this day our daily bread."

Soul food is immensely satisfying and heartwarming, and it brings the entire South under the same banner where the best times are spent around the table. Traditions have deep roots in the South, but there is a need to evaluate and adapt them to current dietary guidelines, and that means reducing calories, fat and sugar in soul food.

The good news is that you can cook comfort food with the right substitutions and not break your diet. By focusing on finding alternatives to carbohydrates, proteins and fats, you can quickly adapt any recipe to your dietary needs.

Substitute Carbs

There are many types of carbs, some are short-molecule simple carbs like sugar and white flour, and others are larger molecules, which cover starches and fiber.

Substitute white bread for whole grain, and experiment with alternative types of flour for breading — almond flour is incredibly versatile. Make

16

use of the wide variety of zero-carb sweeteners we have today, including Aspartame, Saccharin, Sucralose, Stevia and Monk Fruit.

Serve a side of grilled veggies instead of starchy potatoes, and carrots can be a fantastic substitute for yams when cooked to tender and sweet perfection.

Protein Substitutions

Choosing the right proteins can make a significant difference in your calorie and fat intake. Chicken breasts are leaner than thighs and legs, and you can substitute ham for turkey in most recipes. Turkey bacon and Canadian bacon are better alternatives to regular bacon too.

For beef and pork, use lean cuts like tenderloin, round steak, and center-cut pork chops instead of fatty cuts. You might also want to reduce overall meat consumption by adding more fish-based recipes to your meal rotation.

Legumes, including beans — a Southern staple, are extraordinary sources of high-quality proteins, so make good use of them.

Cook Healthier

Adapting soul food to a healthier lifestyle is more than the ingredients; it's how you cook them.

Use vegetable oil instead of lard and steam your veggies instead of grilling them. An air-frier can be an excellent investment that will allow you to cook the crispiest fried chicken with very little oil, and potatoes come out great too! Talking about potatoes, try baking your potatoes and yams instead of deep-frying them. Drizzled with olive oil, they end up golden and crispy.

Salt represents a significant health risk, and you can use less of it without losing flavor by adding more aromatic herbs and spices to your soups and broths.

Soul food is healthier than ever!

With a few ingredient substitutions and fundamental changes in your kitchen, you can cook and share your favorite Southern food reduced in carbs, salt and fat. And that's just the beginning. We're entering the golden era for plant-based meat substitutes, where people use jackfruit instead of shredded pork, lentil patties instead of beef and sausages are made with figs.

Soul food is all about sharing, and sharing is caring, so make sure your cooking is inclusive and suitable to anyone, despite their dietary needs and preferences. That's the real definition of cooking with love.

Old School Recipes

Old-Fashioned recipes are written with simple ingredients. The terminology pinch, lil, and till are classic words used in old school cooking. I wanted to keep the words to represent old school cooking recipes.

Old-fashioned Southern Creamed Corn

How to cook Old-fashioned Southern Creamed Corn

Stewed fresh corn off cob. Shuck corn, take off silks, wash cut off cob, pinch of salt, or substitute, teaspoon of sugar or substitute, lil black pepper teaspoon of flour, optional teaspoon of chopped green bell pepper and a half a teaspoon of self-rising flour, work all ingredients up, place in a skillet with a tablespoon of oil fry on medium with lid, stir occasionally, till start lightly browning, then stir in water till your desired thickness, for cream style corn, let simmer for 15 minutes on low. This recipe is for a dozen of corn off the cob, entire process should take an hour and 15 minutes.

SOUTHERN-STYLE CABBAGE

HOW TO COOK SOUTHERN-STYLE CABBAGE

2 medium heads of cabbages, cut save best outer leaves, cut out heart center, fold leaves pull out center stems dispose, break up cabbage leaves included with green outer leaves, wash thoroughly, place in a pot with 1/3 water with washed uncooked turkey or ham meat, lil crushed Red pepper, teaspoon of sugar or substitute, Add Smoked turkey tails. Boil on Med a half an hour, place 5 potatoes red or white potatoes in with the cabbages and meat, let boil for another half an hour till done.

SOUTHERN-STYLE COLLARDS

HOW TO COOK SOUTHERN-STYLE COLLARDS

I head of collards, cut save best outer leaves, cut out heart center, fold leaves pull out center stems dispose, break up cabbage leaves included with green outer leaves, wash thoroughly, place in a pot with 1/3 water with washed uncooked turkey or ham meat, lil crushed Red pepper, teaspoon of sugar or substitute, Add Smoked turkey tails. Boil on Med a half an hour, place 5 potatoes red or white potatoes in with the cabbages and meat, let boil for another half an hour till done.

MACKEREL PATTIES (Fish cakes)

How to cook MACKEREL PATTIES (Fish cakes)

I pint can of MACKEREL. Drain excess oil., pick and dispose all black outer flesh, place in bowl, pinch of salt or salt substitutes, teaspoon of flour, lightly sprinkle black pepper teaspoon of diced onions, lil Apple cider vinegar, preference colored, mix well. Make flat patties fry in corn oil till done on each side, fry on Med.

Down Home Chitterlings

How to cook Down Home Chitterlings

Gallon uncooked chitterlings, wash thoroughly in baking soda, place in pot 1/3 water lil salt , black pepper, crushed red pepper I/2 cup of vinegar, tablespoon of Texas Pete check occasionally while cooking add water and more vinegar if needed, should take less than 2 hour to cook on Med.

Southern Black-Eyed Peas

How to cook Southern Black-Eyed Peas

Black eye peas, pt. of dry beans wash, place in pot half pot to a pint of dry beans with smoke turkey tails or ham, add a pinch of baking soda, lil black pepper, lil salt or salt substitute boil on Med 1 hour then put a pinch of baking soda let boil for about 15 minutes, cut eye on low, keep check on water in pot and check for not sticking

Old-Fashioned Grated Sweet Potato Pudding

How to cook Old-Fashioned Grated Sweet Potato Pudding

Sweet potatoes pudding, wash peal and hand grate 6 sweet potatoes mix in bowl stick of melted unsalted butter or substitute, half cup of sugar or substitute, teaspoon of all spice, pinch of salt optional tablespoon of fresh milk mix thoroughly place in greased baking pan bake on 350 for an hour.

Southern Fried Sweet Potato Jacks

How to cook Southern Fried Sweet Potato Jacks

Fried sweet potatoes jacks. Prepare rolled dough aside. 6 fresh sweet potatoes washed pealed boil till done drain water place in bowl add teaspoon all spice, pinch of salt teaspoon or substitute half cup sugar or sugar substitute, teaspoon of milk, stick of melted butter or substitute mix all ingredients place a tablespoon of filling in prepared dough, pinch around sides of dough, fry in corn oil on Med, till each side is done.

Southern Fried Chicken

How to cook southern Fried Chicken

Fried chicken. Sprinkle a lil salt and black pepper lightly on each side prior to washing and prepping the chicken. Roll in self-Rising flour all over chicken, shake off excess flour , fry in corn oil on Medium for 20. Minutes

Words Of Inspirations

Let's be careful how we pray and what we pray for.

We must stay connected to God just like a post on a battery.

My Mom used to tell me baby never bite off more than you can chew. At one time I thought she was talking about food, thank God I learned better.

Bad news is that we all are
in deep danger and trouble,
but the good news is that
God is our Refuge.

Just because some of us
are comfortable, let us not
forget those who are not,
sad but things can always
turn around.

Open your heart and let God in! Let the beats beat up the devil.

Let us appreciate and thank God for what we have before we keep asking for more, He knows what we can handle.

Jesus, Jesus, I love to just call your Name, it Rock's the Holy Spirit in me. JESUS!!

We can never repay God enough, just put him first and continue to do His will, more and more each day.

A tool and a stool to work with the first step in the Bible. A solid foundation!

As long as we sit back
and do nothing something
positive in life might not
ever come our way, we have
to do our part also.

Once the devil gets into our brains and hearts, that's when all hell breaks out. Oh trouble!

The Book of James tells us to say what we mean and mean what we say. Amen!

Sometimes in order to move forward in life, one has to make sacrifices. Thankful that I did many times!

If we haven't gotten our house in order, it's best if we do it today. Repent!

It's not just a blessing to be here, it's a miracle.

Let's all of us stop putting off today for tomorrow.

We are all just living in hope!

The devil wants to win our hearts from God. We must always trust and honor, worship and love God if we want salvation.

The devil kills, still and destroys, his plan is to take our minds off the virus. Stay focused and prayed up!

Let's not go to sleep tonight
before we have a little talk
with God.

I don't know about you but what I do know is that when I make a turn I pray that I stay in God's lane. I don't want to get lost. Heaven is my destination, not hell.

Just imagine what this world would be like if we loved and praised God like some do their vehicle.

We called on Jesus and he answered our prayers, witnessed a family that prays together, stays together, say no more.

I don't know about you but what I do know is that regardless of what I might have or what ever happened to me in this life time of mines, my accepting Jesus as my personal Savior is the best thing that ever happened to me.

In order for us to keep our family close with love and support we must do the same first for God. Remember God is a Jealous God.

I don't know about you but
one thing that I do know
is that can't nobody out love
me and do me like Jesus
and I feel the same way.

There might come to a point in our lives that we might decide to start all over again, well if we didn't include God the first time it want work the next time.

Even in the midst of the darkest moment, Jesus is still the light of the world.

Too many are preying on people and not praying for people.

I don't know about anyone else but what I do know is that as long as I have my right mind, breath and blood still running warm in my veins, I will always praise and Worship God.

A Life Guard might save us from drowning but only God can save us from burning in hell.

It's only by the Grace of God that those of us still have the blood running warm in our veins.

Sometimes our lives can be like a missing piece in a puzzle but yet sometimes it's best to leave that piece missing.

Once I stumbled but God didn't let me fall, abused but didn't break, lost but now I'm found blind but now I can see much.

We all must get healed spiritually and mentally even if we never get healed physically. Glory to God.

Before we decide to ever give up, look up first. Witness, I'm still here.

One thing that we all must accept, comprehend and remember, no one can take the place of Almighty God and He will put us in our place one way or the other.

Faith is like holding on to a strong rope, we try so hard for the knots not to come back, therefore we pull tighter and tighter.

Never feel that no one is better than you are, just because they are doing better than you are. Ashes ashes dirt to dirt.

Sometimes in life after you help certain people get on their feet, they will in return walk all over you. Good News if done from the heart God will in return walk with you.

In order to be successful in life we must not leave out, Almighty God, determination, Faith, positive prayer, hardworking and keep in mind a Vision that will make this happen. Glory to God!

I have been guilty of saying my circle is small until I looked and realized that as long as I include Jesus in it, it's bigger than the Universe. Glory to God Almighty!

I'm still holding on, not to Man but to God. (Tight but it's Right)!

Those of us that are still alive, let's not feel as if we are a mistake, each has a purpose and God has a plan and promise.

May all of those that have no choice but to be on the Road any night be protected by God's hedges.

Let's stop falling for the tricks of some people, I feel like this if you didn't positively support and acknowledge me when I was down and out, well don't think that I don't know your game, I want play but I will pray.

My Mom used to tell me if you make your bed hard you would have to lay in it, she was so Right. When I was a Child I thought like a Child but when I became a Woman of God I put away Childish things.

The Holy Spirit woke me up this morning to share this, let's concentrate more on positive thoughts than the negative, the devil thrives off anything that he can destroy us. Trusting in Almighty will always weigh the negatives.

If we can call on Jesus
when we have health,
broken, sick, unemployed,
stressed, in trouble etc.
Why not Honor and
worship Him?

There are 2 plans of Promises, God's and the devil's, the difference is God never breaks a Promise and the devil is full of empty promises. God said it's our choice!

Yes it's a fact that when one door closes God Open's up another, but first be sure thvat it is God that you had accepted as your personal Savior and not the devil, if not greater disasters in that open door.

Only if Humpty Dumpty had fallen off the wall and was told he couldn't be put back together, just imaging if he had only called on God and God would have fixed it.

A lot of things that we might be preparing for but we best be preparing our Hearts! Look around! Glory to God!

We have to be careful around evil people, they seek your weaknesses first, then they approach your joy.

Jesus suffered, hung and nailed feet and hands to the cross, so that our sins will be forgiven and we will have everlasting life. Why is it so hard for some of us to hold his hand and walk with Him?

At this time we might not reach out and touch many of our hands but we still can touch many of our heart's. Positive prayers, love and support!

Sometimes in life when you help some people get on their feet, if you are not careful, you will be the one that the Feet is walking on. God is still in control!

Our Souls has to be nourished with God's Word and if not we will eventually deteriorate. Fact Amen Glory to God!

Some of us are always sitting back waiting for Miracles but yet not thankful for blessings.

Vintage Photos

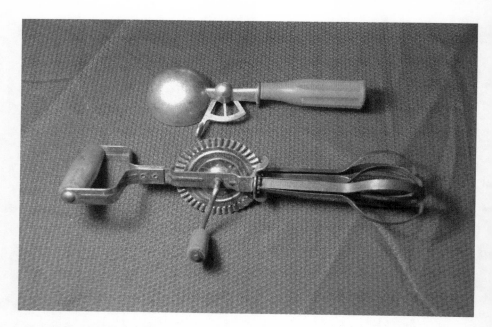

Remembrance of Loved Ones

My Father James "Jim" Bryant

My Mother - Lillie Mae Bryant

My Nephew - Ray Cherry

My Sister - Lillie Bea Knight

Wonderful Friend - Irene Vines Brown

My Great Niece- Latoya Forte

About The Author

Lossie Dupree born and raised in Whitakers, North Carolina. The Daughter of Lillie and James Bryant. She grew up in an old country sharecroppers house in the country of Whitakers, NC. She attended Edgecombe County Public Schools and North Carolina Wesleyan College. Received Associate Degree in Ministry June 2019 from Rhema School of Ministry in Greenville N.C. She attended classes in Ringwood N.C.

She worked 25 years at Gardner's Barbecue 301 Flagship Store in Rocky Mount, NC.

Lossie retired from Southwest Edgecombe High School in Pinetops, North Carolina.

She is very gifted. She has been blessed with many talents; she is a seamstress, caterer, and a floral designer.

Lossie was married to the late Fred Dupree. They had three children: Teresa, Marilyn, and Sandra. Lossie presently lives in Whitakers, North Carolina.

Made in the USA
Middletown, DE
12 October 2023

40658742R00066